Little
Great Chefs®
of Hawai'i
Cookbook

Kaui Philpotts

MUTUAL PUBLISHING

Licensed to Mutual Publishing by
Great Chefs® Television/Publishing
747 Magazine Street
New Orleans , LA 70130
1-800-321-1499
Copyright ©2004

First Printing, July 2004

ISBN 1-56647-675-5
Library of Congress Catalog Card
Number: 2004106979

Mutual Publishing
1215 Center Street, Suite 210
Honolulu, Hawai'i 96816
Telephone (808) 732-1709
Fax (808) 734-4094
e-mail: mutual@lava.net
www.mutualpublishing.com

Design by Joel Shane

Printed in Korea

Table of Contents

Fish and Shellfish

Foreword

When I began writing about food in Hawai'i 20 years ago, I had no idea I'd been assigned to cover the hottest breaking story in the Islands. I'd booked a front-row table just in time for the revolution.

A generation ago there was good food in the Islands, but you had to know where to look—little mom-and-pop restaurants or lunch wagons that sold a cross-cultural mix of entrées on paper plates; or private parties and lū'aus where the buffet table might offer Hawaiian kālua pig and lomilomi salmon, Chinese noodles, Japanese sushi, Vietnamese spring rolls, Filipino lumpia, Korean kalbi and kim chee, and Thai curry.

This was the food we liked and shared amongst ourselves, but it certainly wasn't the food of white table-clothed restaurants—and definitely not the food we served to visitors.

We served visitors what we thought they liked—French onion soup, Caesar salad, chateaubriand, duck à l'orange, chocolate mousse— we flew in frozen sole and served sole almandine. We even served visitors food they thought was Hawaiian, but wasn't—chicken with sliced pineapple and imported fish sprinkled with macadamia nuts. But then, slowly at first, things began to change.

The new resorts brought in highly creative young chefs from all over the world, and Hawai'i began to develop more homegrown talent—chefs from the Islands who knew the local terrain. Hawai'i, the only tropical state, burst with flavors no other part of the country could provide, and these young chefs began exploiting the fresh ingredients found locally, from seafood—'ahi, mahimahi, opah, 'ōpakapaka, shutome, freshwater prawns and cold-water lobster, to produce—fresh herbs on Moloka'i, chocolate on the Big Island, onions on Maui, and baby lettuces on O'ahu.

Hawai'i had one other crucial ingredient—a resident population accustomed to mixing and matching a multitude of Polynesian, Eastern, and Western flavors. It was an audience who responded enthusiastically when a few daring chefs began charring 'ahi with Japanese spices and serving it with a liliko'i sauce, or steaming mahimahi in a combination of Provençal herbs and Hawaiian-style seaweeds.

All the tastes cultivated over the years in secret were out of the closet. Better yet, they were in those white table-clothed restaurants.

Hawai'i went food crazy. New restaurants sprang up. Menus changed daily. Going out for dinner became an adventure. Dozens of chefs, emboldened, cooked up their own versions of Hawaiian cuisine. And everyone who took pleasure in great food profited—including visitors to the Islands, who didn't want sole almandine after all.

Great Chefs® has done a tremendous job, first of finding this culinary revolution in the middle of the Pacific, and then documenting it so beautifully. And I have to salute my friend Kaui Philpotts for having written such an enjoyable book.

Just reading the names of the recipes, you can feel the warm sun, hear the tradewinds, and almost taste paradise.

Aloha. Enjoy.
John Heckathorn, Editor
Honolulu Magazine

Introduction

Think Hawaiian food, and you may recall a tale of culinary horror from a neighbor who attended a lūʻau for tourists at a Waikīkī resort hotel. But there's a lot more to Island food than this, and thanks to young chefs who have incorporated Asian, Hawaiian and EuroAmerican cuisines, a revolution nothing short of phenomenal has changed fine dining in the Islands.

The first Hawaiians arrived about 2000 years ago. In their voyaging canoes they brought their staples: kalo (taro root), ʻulu (breadfruit), ʻuala (sweet potato), puaʻa (pigs), moa (chicken), kukui (candlenut tree), coconuts, and bananas. In these isolated islands, water was sweet, fish abundant, and limu (seaweed) and ʻopihi (shellfish) readily found. Hawaiians added the hōʻiʻo fern, taro leaves (lūʻau) and its crimson stalks (hāhā) to their diet. The men prepared the food, cooking it in imu—fire pits lined with hot volcanic rock. Religious significance was placed on certain foods, such as bananas, coconuts, pork, and shark's meat, which women were forbidden to eat on the threat of death. Men and women dined separately, and many other strict rules of conduct, called kapu, directed their lives.

This changed in 1819, when the great Queen Ka'ahumanu, regent and widow of Kamehameha I, ate a meal with her son and heir, Liholiho, in public, thus ending the kapu against men and women eating at the same table.

The arrival of the first Protestant missionaries from New England in March 1820 brought more changes to Hawai'i. The New England missionaries and other early settlers from Europe combined the foods of their homelands with what was available locally. Many of the earliest settlers married Hawaiian women and stayed in the Islands, further blending dietary habits.

By the middle of the nineteenth century, more foreigners settled in the Islands and with them came sugarcane and pineapple plantations. A need for cheap field labor developed. The Native Hawaiian population had declined in alarming numbers, mostly due to disease, and Hawaiians, while hardworking, were not accustomed to cultivating the land for the profit of others. Waves of immigrant laborers were brought in from China, Japan, Korea, the Philippines, Puerto Rico, and the Portuguese Islands. With them came their cuisines.

Plantation families imported what they could from back home and adapted traditional recipes to what they could get in Hawai'i. Families gathered limu (seaweed), 'opihi (limpets), and fish from the ocean, and cultivated gardens. The Chinese planted lychee and star fruit (carambola); the Japanese grew turnips (daikon) for their pickles; the Koreans raised cabbage and chilies for their kim chee; and the Portuguese brought backyard stone ovens for making bread and bean soups. By the 1930s, the Islands had a distinct local cuisine that blended the foods of the different ethnic groups.

Restaurants and hotels, however, ignored "local food" and served dishes that reflected the tastes of the mainland United States and Europe. At great expense, foods were flown in for fine dining. Local food was considered too ethnic, unsophisticated, and definitely inferior.

But then things changed. Younger chefs who came to oversee the kitchens of the new resorts that popped up in the 1970s and 1980s became interested in local tastes.

The result was the kind of food featured in this book: dishes using fresh island ingredients and combining the diverse cuisines of the many cultures found in Hawai'i.

This book features recipes from Hawai'i's finest restaurant and resort chefs who appear on the Great Chefs® of Hawai'i television series. All the recipes have been revised and tested for the home cook. We urge you to prepare these dishes for your family and friends. We know you will be surprised and delighted.

Native Hawaiians have an expression—Hele mai a'i—"Come here and eat"—and traditionally extended this greeting to friends, family, and even total strangers. We hope you will use this book, then call your friends and neighbors and say, "Hele mai a'i."

Appetizers

There is no better way to sample the complex flavors of Hawaiian cuisine than to graze through the appetizer courses on any island restaurant menu. The same goes for using this book. Chefs are often at their most creative in developing appetizers. Here you will find Asian sauces and dressings with wasabi and chilis, and smoked and seared fish with fresh fruit sauces.

Alan Wong *Alan Wong's Restaurant, Honolulu, O'ahu*

'Ahi Cake

Serves 8

A Hawaiian version of a terrine, this 'ahi cake combines the color and flavor of sweet Maui onion, eggplant, and seared 'ahi tuna.

INGREDIENTS

1 garlic clove

1 teaspoon minced fresh rosemary

3 fresh thyme sprigs

1 cup olive oil

4 Maui or other sweet white onions, cut into 1/4-inch-thick crosswise slices

4 Japanese eggplants, cut into 1/4-inch-thick diagonal slices

Salt and freshly ground pepper to taste

8 ounces sashimi-grade 'ahi tuna, cut into 1/4-inch-thick vertical slices

4 vine-ripened tomatoes, cut into paper-thin slices

8 basil leaves

PREPARATION

Put the garlic, rosemary, and thyme in a blender or food processor and purée. With the motor running, gradually add the oil. Set aside. Preheat the broiler. Sprinkle the onions and eggplant on both sides with salt and pepper and place on a dish for 15 minutes to sweat. Pat the vegetables dry with paper towels. Place the vegetables on a grill pan and brush on both sides with the garlic-herb olive oil. Broil the vegetables 3 inches from the heat until they are lightly browned, about 2 minutes. Refrigerate. Sprinkle the 'ahi with salt and pepper. Heat a large sauté pan or skillet over high heat, coat the pan with the garlic-herb oil, and sear the 'ahi slices for 15 seconds on each side, or until the outside is cooked and the center is still rare. Transfer the 'ahi to a plate and refrigerate.

TO ASSEMBLE

Fan half the tomato slices in a circular pattern around the bottom of a 6-cup bowl lined with plastic wrap. Layer half of the onions, basil leaves, and eggplant at the bottom of the dish. Drizzle with 1 tablespoon of the garlic-herb olive oil. Place half of the 'ahi slices over the vegetables. You may have to cut and piece 'ahi together to form an even layer. Repeat this process to make a second layer of vegetables, infused oil, and seared fish. For the last layer, fan the remaining tomatoes in a circular pattern over the top of the vegetables. Place a small plate upside down on top of the tomatoes and weight with a heavy, small dish or other object. Refrigerate for 1 hour.

TO SERVE

Drain the juices from the 'ahi cake. Unmold the 'ahi cake, carefully slice it into 8 even portions, and serve.

OnJin Kim   OnJin's Cafe, Honolulu, O'ahu

Charred Sichimi 'Ahi Coated with Japanese Spices with Liliko'i-Soy Sauce

Serves 4

Japanese flavors predominate in a simple dish of seared 'ahi with greens. The liliko'i-soy sauce adds the island touch.

INGREDIENTS

1/2 Maui or other sweet white onion, finely sliced

1/2 teaspoon fresh lemon juice

1/2 daikon, cut into julienne

1/2 carrot, peeled and cut into fine julienne

12 ounces 'ahi tuna

3 tablespoons shichimi

1/2 tablespoon olive oil

Liliko'i-Soy Sauce

1 cup dry white wine

1/4 cup unsweetened liliko'i (passion fruit) purée or
    passion fruit concentrate

1 shallot, sliced

6 white peppercorns

1 bay leaf

1 tablespoon soy sauce

1 tablespoon sugar

1 cup heavy (whipping) cream

1/2 cup (1 stick) unsalted butter, cut into tablespoon-
    sized pieces

Garnish

4 shiso leaves, stemmed

4 pieces pickled ginger, drained

continued on next page

PREPARATION

Toss the onion with the lemon juice. Place the daikon in cold water to crisp for 15 minutes. Drain the daikon and mix with the carrot. Set aside.

TO PREPARE THE 'AHI

Cut the 'ahi 1-1/2 inches thick, then into rectangles about 6 inches long. Coat the fillets with shichimi. In a heavy, large sauce pan or skillet over high heat, heat the olive oil until just before smoking. Cook a batch of 'ahi for about 10 seconds on each side, or until seared on the outside and rare on the inside. Using a slotted spatula, transfer to paper towels. Repeat to cook the remaining 'ahi. Slice the 'ahi against the grain into 1/8-inch-thick pieces.

TO MAKE THE SAUCE

In a medium saucepan, combine the white wine, liliko'i purée, shallot, peppercorns, bay leaf, soy sauce, and sugar. If using sweetened passion fruit juice concentrate, omit the sugar.

Bring to a boil over medium heat and cook until reduced to 1/4 cup. Add the cream and continue to cook to reduce to 1/2 cup. Remove from heat and whisk in the butter, one piece at a time. Keep warm over hot water until ready to use.

TO SERVE

Place 1/2 teaspoon of the sliced onion in the middle of each plate. Mound 1 tablespoon daikon mixture on top. Place 1 shiso leaf on the top of each plate and set 1 piece of the ginger on the leaf. Ladle 2 tablespoons of sauce around the daikon on the bottom third of each plate. Lean the 'ahi against the daikon on top of the sauce.

Roy Yamaguchi   *Roy's Restaurant, Honolulu, O'ahu*

Kona Shrimp Lumpia with Spicy Mango Sauce

Serves 4

No appetizer has ever tasted as good as this new twist on the old-fashioned egg roll. Frozen extra-thin lumpia wrappers work well, and you won't be able to get enough of the spicy mango sauce.

INGREDIENTS

Lumpia Filling

6 ounces cellophane noodles

3 ounces fresh shiitake mushrooms, stemmed and diced, or 1 ounce dried shiitakes, soaked in warm water for 30 minutes

2 tablespoons Asian sesame oil

1 cup finely chopped Chinese mustard cabbage or napa cabbage

1 teaspoon minced fresh cilantro

1 teaspoon minced fresh ginger

1 teaspoon minced garlic

1 green onion, including some of the green top, minced

3 fresh water chestnuts, finely diced

1 pound shrimp, chopped

1 to 2 tablespoons Thai fish sauce (nam pla)

5 tablespoons water

2 tablespoons cornstarch, plus cornstarch for dusting

12 lumpia wrappers

Spicy Mango Sauce

1/4 cup Thai chili paste or any sweet chili paste

1 cup sake

1/4 cup liliko'i (passion fruit) purée, or orange juice concentrate

1/4 teaspoon minced fresh ginger

1/4 teaspoon minced garlic

1 teaspoon minced shallot

1 mango, peeled, cut from the pit, and finely diced

Garnish

2 teaspoons white sesame seeds, toasted

4 teaspoons snipped fresh chives

1/4 mango, peeled, cut from the pit, and cut into julienne

TO MAKE THE LUMPIA

In a large pot, bring salted water to a boil. Add the noodles and cook for 1 minute, or until just tender. Drain and set aside.

If using dried shiitakes, drain and squeeze them dry, reserving the soaking liquid for another use. Dice the mushrooms. In a skillet over medium-high heat, heat the sesame oil and sauté the mushrooms, cabbage, cilantro, ginger, garlic, green onion, water chestnuts, and cooked noodles for 1 minute. Let cool, then combine with the shrimp and fish sauce.

Mix the water and 2 tablespoons cornstarch in a small bowl. Lay the lumpia wrappers on a work surface and brush the edges of the wrappers with the cornstarch mixture. Place 2 tablespoons filling in a line on the front edge of each wrapper, leaving a 1/2-inch border. Fold the edge of the wrapper nearest you over the filling, then fold in the sides and roll the wrapper into a cylinder. Seal the ends and dust with cornstarch. In a large sauté pan or skillet over high heat, heat the oil until very hot and fry the lumpia, 4 at a time, for about 45 seconds on each side or until golden

continued on next page

brown. Repeat with the remaining lumpia. Remove with tongs and drain on paper towels. Keep warm.

TO MAKE THE MANGO SAUCE

Combine all the ingredients in a medium saucepan. Simmer over low heat for 15 minutes. Strain through a fine-meshed sieve. Set aside and keep warm.

TO SERVE

Pool 1/4 cup of the warm sauce on each of 6 salad plates. Place 2 lumpia on top of the sauce and garnish with the sesame seeds, chives, and mango.

Amy Ferguson-Ota   Oodles of Noodles, Kailua-Kona, Hawai'i

Puna Goat Cheese and Vegetable Terrine

Makes one 8-by-1/2-inch terrine

Great chefs in Hawai'i and the world over use the finest local products — in this case, goat cheese made in the Puna district of the Big Island. The goat cheese between each layer helps bind this terrine.

INGREDIENTS

3 ounces fresh shiitake mushrooms, stemmed and sliced, or 1 ounce dried shiitakes, soaked in hot water for 30 minutes

6 large Japanese eggplants, sliced lengthwise into 1/4-inch slices

3 large zucchini, sliced lengthwise into 1/4-inch slices

1 medium yellow squash, sliced crosswise into 1/4-inch slices

1 Maui or other sweet white onion, finely diced

12 garlic cloves

Olive oil for brushing and sprinkling

Salt to taste

10 ounces crumbled Puna or other fresh white goat cheese

3 red bell peppers, roasted, peeled, and seeded

1 tablespoon chopped basil leaves

1 cup white mushrooms, sliced

1 ripe tomato, peeled and seeded

Balsamic vinegar for sprinkling

Freshly ground black pepper to taste

8 sprigs of fresh basil

To make the terrine

Preheat the oven to 350°F. If using dried shiitakes, drain them, reserving the soaking liquid for another use. Salt the eggplant slices and let sit for 30 minutes; rinse with cold water. Arrange the shiitakes, eggplants, zucchini, squash, onion, and garlic on an oiled baking sheet. Brush with olive oil and sprinkle with salt. Roast for 10 minutes. Set aside and cool. Squeeze half of the garlic cloves out of the skins and chop.

Line a 2-quart loaf pan, terrine, or triangular mold with plastic wrap, leaving 4 inches of plastic wrap hanging over each edge of the pan. Arrange the vegetables in the pan.

Lay the eggplant and zucchini slices across the pan, alternating the vegetables and overlapping the slices to form a continuous layer. Sprinkle with onion. Using your fingers or the back of a spoon, spread a thin layer of cheese on top of the onion. Top with a layer of peppers and a layer of basil. Top with a thin layer of cheese. Sprinkle with mushrooms and the chopped garlic and top with another layer of cheese. Place the squash slices over the cheese. Put the tomatoes over the squash and top with basil. Press down gently with your fingers. Fold the plastic wrap over the top of the mold, and refrigerate for 3 hours.

TO SERVE
Lift the mold out of the pan. Slice through the plastic with a serrated knife. Peel off the plastic and arrange a slice on each chilled plate. Sprinkle with olive oil, balsamic vinegar, and pepper. Garnish with a sprig of basil and the unpeeled roasted garlic cloves.

Soups
& Salads

Salads and hot climates go hand in hand. Hawai'i chefs have given the simple green salad new meaning by incorporating crisp wonton wrappers, macadamia nuts, and fresh raw 'ahi. The dressings are innovative: the vinaigrettes use such ingredients as sesame oil, chili paste, and lime juice and can be used on salads and vegetable dishes of your own design.

Island soups are just as fresh and bright, making use of local vegetables and styles.

Mark Ellman   *Maui Tacos, Lāhainā, Maui*

'Ahi and Taro Salad
Serves 4

Raw 'ahi, taro root, macadamia nuts, and a spike of chili pepper water are molded into a colorful salad topped with two colors of tobiko or caviar. A purée of cilantro and macadamia nut oil adds a piquant flavor note.

8 ounces taro root, peeled and cut into 1/2-inch cubes

Cilantro Purée
4 cups packed fresh cilantro leaves
2 cups macadamia nut oil or walnut oil
Salt and freshly ground pepper to taste
12 ounces sashimi-grade 'ahi tuna, cut into 1/2-inch cubes
1 garlic clove, minced
1/2 Maui or other sweet white onion, minced
1 carrot, chopped
1 beet, peeled and cut into fine julienne
1 cup macadamia nuts, finely chopped
2 teaspoons minced fresh ginger
1 cup soy sauce
2 teaspoons Asian sesame oil
1/4 cup finely chopped ogo (seaweed)
4 teaspoons chili pepper water (see recipe below)
1/4 cup diced macadamia nuts, toasted
4 teaspoons white sesame seeds, toasted
1/2 cup black tobiko or salmon caviar
1/2 cup green tobiko

Chili Pepper Water (makes 3 cups)
2-1/2 cups boiling water
3/4 cup cold water
2 tablespoons distilled white vinegar
1 garlic clove, minced
1 tablespoon chopped fresh ginger
14 Hawaiian or Thai chilies

TO MAKE THE CHILI PEPPER WATER

In a blender or food processor, combine all ingredients and purée until smooth, about 1 minute. Pour into hot sterilized bottles, cover, and refrigerate.

TO COOK THE TARO

Scrub the outside of the taro root with a brush. Put in a saucepan with enough boiling salted water to cover the taro. Cover and simmer for 1-1/2 hours, or until tender. Remove the taro, drain, and let cool. With a sharp knife, remove the outer peel and cut into cubes.

TO MAKE THE CILANTRO PURÉE

In a blender or food processor, combine the cilantro and oil and purée. Stir in the salt and pepper. Set aside. In a large bowl, combine all the remaining ingredients except the tobiko or salmon caviar. Toss and let sit for 15 minutes. Line a baking pan with parchment paper or aluminum foil. Place four 4-inch ring molds on the prepared baking pan. Divide the salad among the molds and gently pack down to firm. Refrigerate for at least 1 hour.

TO SERVE

Lift the rings with a spatula and place on plates. Run the tip of a small sharp knife around the molds to loosen, and lift the molds. Pour one fourth of the purée around each salad mold. Top each salad with a teaspoon of black tobiko and 1/2 teaspoon of green tobiko, or spoon the caviar on top.

Peter Merriman   *Merriman's Bamboo Bistro, Wailuku, Hawai'i*

Grilled Shrimp and Star Fruit Salad

Serves 4

Spicy and exotic are the best words to describe this colorful and attractive salad. If star fruit is difficult to find, mango makes a wonderful substitute.

INGREDIENTS

1/4 cup olive oil

2 tablespoons minced shallots

2 tablespoons minced fresh cilantro

Salt and freshly ground pepper to taste

16 to 20 large shrimp, peeled with head left on

1 tablespoon minced fresh ginger

1/2 cup fresh lime juice

1/8 teaspoon red pepper flakes

2 tablespoons chopped fresh mint

1 ripe star fruit, sliced thin

4 handfuls (4 ounces) watercress or arugula sprigs

PREPARATION

In a nonaluminum baking dish, combine the oil, shallots, cilantro, salt, and pepper. Skewer 4 or 5 shrimp on each of 4 sets of parallel skewers, running the skewer through the head and tail of each shrimp and leaving space between shrimp. Marinate at room temperature for 1 hour, or cover and refrigerate for up to 8 hours. Let the shrimp sit at room temperature for 30 minutes before cooking.

Light a fire in a charcoal or gas grill, or preheat the broiler. Combine the ginger, lime juice, pepper flakes, mint, and star fruit in a small bowl; toss to mix. Grill or broil the shrimp for 1 minute on each side, or until pink. Set aside. Make a bed of watercress or arugula on each of 4 salad plates and place one fourth of the star fruit mixture on top of each. Take the shrimp off the skewers and place 4 or 5 on top of each salad.

Thomas B. H. Wong *The Surf Room, Royal Hawaiian Waikīkī
Sheraton, Honolulu, Oʻahu*

Togarashi Seared Beef Poke with Chilled Spicy Tomato Soup

Serves 4

Poke is traditionally a mix of raw diced fish, onions, limu (seaweed), and Hawaiian salt; however, this variation using sautéed beef is very good. If prepared in advance, the flavors have an even better chance to meld into a spicy and delicious dish. Prepared togarashi spice mix, found at Asian markets, can be used if you prefer.

INGREDIENTS

Togarashi Spice Mix

1-1/2 teaspoons cayenne pepper

1-1/2 teaspoons paprika

1 teaspoon red pepper flakes

1 teaspoon ground pepper

1 teaspoon white sesame seeds, toasted

1 teaspoon black sesame seeds

1 teaspoon cumin seeds, toasted

1 teaspoon mustard seeds, toasted

1 pound beef sirloin, cut into 1/2-inch dice

2 tablespoons peanut oil

Poke Sauce

1/2 Maui or other sweet white onion, diced

1 garlic clove, minced

1 tomato, seeded and diced

Minced fresh cilantro to taste

Chili pepper water to taste

1 tablespoon soy sauce

1 teaspoon Hawaiian or kosher salt

1 teaspoon patis fish sauce

Chilled Spicy Tomato Soup *(recipe follows)*

Garnish

2 green onions, cut into julienne including some green
    tops for garnish

continued on next page

Grind all the spice mix ingredients in a spice grinder. Season the beef with the togarashi spice mix. In a sauté pan or skillet over high heat, heat the oil and sauté the beef until it is seared on the outside and rare on the inside, about 2 minutes. Remove the meat from the pan and refrigerate it for 1 hour. Add all the remaining ingredients except the soup to the seared beef and mix well. Taste and adjust the seasoning.

TO SERVE

Ladle 1/4 of the tomato soup into each dish. Place a portion of the beef poke in the center of the soup and garnish with the green onion.

Chilled Spicy Tomato Soup

1/2 cup olive oil

1 Maui or other sweet white onion, cut into 1/2-inch dice

2 garlic cloves, coarsely chopped

4 vine-ripened tomatoes, quartered

1/2 cup tarragon vinegar

1-1/2 teaspoons chili pepper water

3 tablespoons fish sauce, preferably Tiparos® brand

PREPARATION

In a saucepan over medium heat, heat 1/4 cup of the oil and sauté the onion and garlic. Add the tomatoes and simmer 2 to 3 minutes, until all the ingredients are tender. Transfer to a blender and purée. With the machine running, gradually add the remaining oil, then the vinegar, chili water, and fish sauce. Cover and refrigerate for 2 to 3 hours before serving.

Meat
& Poultry

Although fruits and vegetables are playing a larger role in most people's diet and are an important focus for chefs as well, meat and poultry remain favorites with most diners.

Here, you'll find main-course basics with a Hawaiian lilt, like lamb chops with ginger cream and blackened chicken with banana-rum sauce.

George Mavrothalassitis   *Chef Mavro, Honolulu, O'ahu*

Beef Tenderloin and Poached Oysters with Essence of Pinot Noir and Chervil Sauce

Serves 4

The silky texture and fresh taste of oysters pair with the beef tenderloins. The rich wine sauce and piquant chervil sauce add the perfect contrasts to this surf-and-turf variation.

INGREDIENTS

4 tablespoons olive oil

4 6-ounce beef tenderloin fillets

2 bunches spinach, well washed and stemmed

4 large fresh oysters, shucked

Essence of Pinot Noir

2 tablespoons olive oil

1 Maui onion or other sweet white onion, finely sliced

1 bottle Pinot Noir wine

1/2 cup carrot, peeled and chopped

Salt and freshly ground pepper to taste

Chervil Sauce

2 tablespoons extra-virgin olive oil

1 onion, finely sliced

1 cup dry white wine

1/2 cup minced fresh chervil

Salt and freshly ground pepper to taste

TO PREPARE THE FILLETS

Preheat the oven to 350°F. In a large sauté pan or skillet over medium-high heat, heat 2 tablespoons of the olive oil and cook the fillets for 3 to 4 minutes on each side. Bake for 6 to 7 minutes for medium rare.

Place the spinach in the top of a steamer and place the oysters on the spinach. Steam the spinach and oysters over

continued on next page

boiling water in a medium, covered pot for 3 to 4 minutes, until the oysters have firmed. With a spoon, set the oysters aside on a plate. Drain the spinach well. In a large saucepan over medium heat, heat the remaining 2 tablespoons of olive oil and sauté the spinach for 2 minutes. Set aside.

TO MAKE THE ESSENCE

In a medium saucepan on low heat, heat the olive oil and sauté the onion for 10 minutes. Add one third of the wine and cook to reduce until almost dry. Add another third of the wine and cook to reduce again until almost dry. Add the last third of the wine and cook to reduce by half. Strain, reserving the onion.

In a steamer over boiling water, steam the carrots for 5 minutes, or until tender. Remove and put in a blender or food processor with a little water reserved from the steamer. Purée until smooth. Add the carrot purée to the sauce. Simmer the sauce for 10 minutes. Purée in a blender or food processor until very smooth. Add salt and pepper.

TO MAKE THE CHERVIL SAUCE

In a medium saucepan over low heat, heat the olive oil and sauté the onion for 3 minutes, or until translucent. Add the white wine and simmer for 25 minutes. In a food processor or blender, combine the onion mixture and chervil. Purée to a smooth sauce. Add salt and pepper.

TO SERVE

Make a bed of spinach in the center of each plate. Top with a fillet. Top the fillet with one fourth of the reserved onion. Place 1 oyster on the onions. Surround with essence of Pinot Noir and cover the oyster with chervil sauce.

Beverly Gannon   Hāliʻimaile General Store, Hāliʻimaile, Maui

Blackened Jawaiian Spice Chicken Breasts with Banana-Rum Sauce and Chili Corn Cakes

Serves 4

Blackened Jawaiian chicken combines a Caribbean influence with Hawaiian ingredients in this dish. The term Jawaiian comes out of the island surf culture and denotes a blending of Jamaican reggae and Hawaiian influences in food, music, and lifestyle.

INGREDIENTS

Jawaiian Spice Mix

2 tablespoons ground allspice
2 tablespoons ground cinnamon
2 teaspoons dried thyme
2 teaspoons dried rosemary
2 teaspoons dried chives
1 teaspoon salt
1 teaspoon sugar
2 teaspoons dried onion
8 boneless skinless chicken breast halves
6 tablespoons clarified butter

Banana-Rum Sauce

2 tablespoons butter
1/2 cup chopped onion
1/2 cup chopped celery
2 garlic cloves, minced
4 bananas, cut into 1/2-inch pieces
2-1/2 cups chicken stock
1/2 cup sake
1/2 vanilla bean, halved lengthwise
Juice of 2 limes
3 star anise pods
1/2 cup rum

Chili Corn Cakes

1-1/4 cups milk
2 tablespoons butter, melted
3 eggs

3/4 cup unbleached all-purpose flour

1/2 cup cornmeal

1/2 teaspoon baking powder

1/2 teaspoon baking soda

1/2 teaspoon salt

1 teaspoon sugar

1 cup fresh or frozen corn kernels

1/2 cup diced peeled green chilies

Peanut oil for frying

Fresh thyme sprigs for garnish

TO MAKE THE SPICE MIX AND BLACKEN THE CHICKEN

Combine all the spice ingredients and mix well. Preheat the oven to 350°F. Heat a large cast-iron skillet over high heat until smoking. Coat the chicken breasts with the spice mix. Add to the pan. Drizzle butter over the top of the breasts. Cook for 3 minutes, or until blackened on the bottom. Turn and drizzle more butter on the other side and blacken for another 3 minutes. Bake for about 10 minutes, or until done.

TO MAKE THE BANANA-RUM SAUCE

In a medium saucepan, melt the butter over medium heat and sauté the onions and celery for 2 minutes, or until the onion is translucent. Add the garlic and cook for 1 minute. Add the bananas and cook until they begin to caramelize. Add the stock, sake, vanilla bean, lime juice, and star anise, and simmer for 10 minutes. Remove the vanilla bean and star anise. Put the banana mixture into a blender or food processor and purée. Return to the saucepan and add the rum. Cook over medium heat for 2 minutes, or until thickened. Strain through a sieve. *continued on next page*

TO MAKE THE CORN CAKES

In a large bowl, beat the milk, butter, and eggs together. In a small bowl, stir the flour, cornmeal, baking powder, baking soda, salt, and sugar together. Add the dry ingredients to the wet ingredients. Stir just to combine. Gently blend in the corn and chilies.

In a large cast-iron skillet over medium heat, heat just enough oil to film the bottom of the pan. Add 1/4 cup batter for each cake. Cook for 1 to 2 minutes on each side, or until golden brown. Repeat to cook the remaining batter. Remove to a plate and keep warm.

TO SERVE

Ladle some sauce onto each plate and place a chicken breast on top. Cut the corn cakes in half and place one half on each side of the chicken. Garnish with thyme.

Mark Ellman *Maui Tacos, Lāhainā, Maui*

Indonesian Grilled Lamb Chops with Ginger Cream

Serves 4

Kecap manis, a dark, sweet Indonesian soy sauce, gives these lamb chops a unique flavor. The ginger cream and basil purée balance the dish beautifully. The lamb marinates for 24 hours.

INGREDIENTS

Marinade

2 cups kecap manis

2 cups minced peeled fresh ginger

1/4 cup minced garlic

1/4 cup Asian sesame oil

1 cup minced fresh mint

1/2 cup whole-grain mustard

2 pounds lamb loin chops, trimmed and sliced

Ginger Cream

4 cups heavy (whipping) cream

1/2 cup sliced peeled fresh ginger

Salt and freshly ground pepper to taste

Basil Purée

2 cups fresh basil leaves

2 cups olive oil

Salt and freshly ground pepper to taste

2 roasted garlic cloves

Garnish

8 asparagus tips, blanched

4 tablespoons pickled ginger

White sesame seeds for sprinkling

TO MAKE THE MARINADE

In a shallow nonaluminum container, combine all the marinade ingredients and mix. Add the lamb chops, turn to coat them, cover, and refrigerate for at least 24 hours. Remove the lamb from the refrigerator 45 minutes before grilling. Light a fire in a charcoal grill or preheat a gas grill. Grill the lamb over a hot fire for 6 to 7 minutes on each side for medium-rare.

TO MAKE THE GINGER CREAM

In a small saucepan, combine the cream and ginger. Cook over medium-low heat until reduced by half, or until the mixture coats the back of a spoon. Add salt and pepper. Set aside and keep warm.

TO MAKE THE BASIL PURÉE

Purée all the ingredients in a blender or food processor, in batches if necessary.

TO SERVE

Lace each plate with ginger cream and place one fourth of the lamb chops on top. Sprinkle with asparagus tips and pickled ginger, then drizzle with basil purée and scatter sesame seeds on top.

Fish &Shellfish

Thanks to the chefs of the new Hawaiian cuisine and the efforts of the State of Hawai'i, a wide variety of reef and deepwater fish such as opah, kajiki, marlin, shark, and kūmū are now as popular in island cooking as the more familiar onaga, 'ōpakapaka, and 'ahi tuna. Many of Hawai'i's chefs draw from Asian techniques such as steaming and searing with hot oil, and smoking. Both recipes and techniques are adaptable to stateside fish, and substitutes are given.

Beverly Gannon   *Hāli'imaile General Store, Hāli'imaile, Maui*

Portuguese Steamed Clams
Serves 6

Inspired by the heritage of the Upcountry region of Maui,
this dish combines clams and sausage with Pacific Rim
seasonings of fresh ginger, chili paste, sake, and cilantro.

INGREDIENTS

2 tablespoons olive oil

1 tablespoon minced garlic

1/2 cup minced fresh ginger

2 onions, finely chopped

3 red bell peppers, seeded, deribbed, and finely chopped

8 ounces mild Portuguese sausage (linguiça), cut into
   1/4-inch chunks

1-1/2 cups sake

6 cups reduced fish stock or clam juice

1-1/2 tablespoons Chinese chili paste

2 tomatoes, peeled, seeded, and coarsely diced

5 dozen clams, scrubbed

1/2 cup fresh cilantro sprigs, chopped

PREPARATION

In a large pot over medium heat, heat the oil, and sauté the
garlic, onions, and red peppers for 2 minutes, or until
translucent. Add the sausage and sauté for 5 minutes, or until
the sausage is slightly browned. Add the sake and stir to
scrape up the browned bits from the bottom of the pan. Add
the fish stock or clam broth and cook until reduced by half.
Add the chili paste, tomatoes, and clams. Cover and cook until
the clams open, approximately 6 to 8 minutes. Discard any
clams that do not open. Ladle the clams and broth into bowls
and garnish with cilantro.

Jean-Marie Josselin   *A Pacific Café, Kapaʻa, Kauaʻi*

Salmon and Shrimp Gyoza with Sweet Chili Vinaigrette and Sweet Chili Beurre Blanc

Serves 4

Gyoza are Japanese fried dumplings, enjoyed alone or with noodles at lunch, dinner, or as a snack. This contemporary version has a filling of salmon and shrimp, and is served with a rich lime-ginger sauce.

INGREDIENTS

Lime-Ginger Sauce Base

1 cup dry white wine

2-1/2 teaspoons minced fresh ginger

1 cup heavy (whipping) cream

1 cup (2 sticks) cold, unsalted butter, cut into tablespoon-sized pieces

Juice of 1 lime

Salt and freshly ground pepper to taste

Thai Chili Vinaigrette

3/4 cup olive oil

2 tablespoons mirin or sweet sherry

1/2 cup rice wine vinegar

1 tablespoon minced fresh cilantro

Salt and freshly ground pepper to taste

Filling

8 medium shrimp

8 to 10 ounces salmon fillet, skinned

1 egg

1/2 cup Thai chili paste

Salt and freshly ground pepper to taste

1/2 red bell pepper, seeded, deribbed, and diced

1 fresh cilantro sprig, chopped

Gyoza

1 tablespoon cornstarch, plus cornstarch for dusting

2 tablespoons water

16 large dim sum or wonton wrappers

Filling, as previous

1 cup peanut oil for frying

1 tablespoon minced fresh cilantro

1 tablespoon Thai chili paste

4 fresh basil sprigs, stemmed and chopped

1/2 cup extra-virgin olive oil

1 cup shredded Chinese cabbage

2 red bell peppers, seeded, deribbed, and cut into julienne

1 fresh cilantro sprig, stemmed and chopped

1/2 cup oyster sauce

1/2 cup Thai chili paste

1 tablespoon minced fresh cilantro

8 fresh flowers

TO MAKE THE SAUCE BASE

In a medium, heavy saucepan, combine the wine and ginger and bring to a boil. Reduce heat to medium and cook to reduce to about 1/2 cup. Add the cream and cook to reduce to 1 cup. Reduce heat to low and whisk in the butter 1 piece at a time. Remove the pan from heat as necessary to keep the sauce base just warm enough to melt each piece of butter. Add the lime juice, salt, and pepper. Keep warm over tepid water for up to 1 hour.

TO MAKE THE VINAIGRETTE

In blender or food processor, combine all ingredients and purée. Place in a squeeze bottle and refrigerate.

continued on next page

TO MAKE THE FILLING

Reserve 3 shrimp. In a blender or food processor, combine the salmon, the remaining shrimp, the egg, chili paste, and seasoning. Purée until smooth. Cut the reserved 3 shrimp into small pieces and stir into the mixture with the red bell pepper and cilantro.

TO MAKE THE GYOZA

Mix the cornstarch with the water and moisten the edges of the wonton wrappers. Place 1 tablespoon of the filling in the center of a wrapper. With your fingers bring one point across the filling at an angle to the opposite corner, making 2 offset triangles. Grasp both outer points and pull around behind the filling, overlapping slightly. Press the ends together and dust the gyoza with cornstarch. Repeat with remaining wrappers. Bring a large pot of salted water to a boil and drop in the gyoza. Cook for 2 minutes, then remove with a slotted spoon and drain on paper towels.

In a large sauté pan or skillet over medium-high heat, heat the oil to 350°F, or until it ripples. Add the gyoza and cook for 1 minute, until the edges are crisp.

TO FINISH THE SAUCE

Put the sauce base, cilantro, and chili paste in a blender or food processor and purée.

In a blender or food processor, combine the basil and oil and purée until smooth. Put in a squeeze bottle.

TO SERVE

Pool one fourth of the sauce on a serving plate. Toss the Chinese cabbage, peppers, and cilantro with the Thai chili vinaigrette and mound one fourth in the center of the sauce. Place 4 gyoza in a radial pattern on the greens. Put the oyster sauce and the Thai chili paste in separate squeeze bottles. Drizzle oyster sauce, basil purée, and Thai chili paste over the entire dish. Garnish with a sprinkle of cilantro and 2 fresh flowers. Repeat with remaining dishes.

Russell Siu   *3660 on the Rise, Honolulu, O'ahu*

Jasmine Tea-Steamed Fillet of 'Ōpakapaka with Coriander-Butter Sauce

Serves 4

Ginger brightens the crust on these fish fillets, coated with a silken cream reduction sauce. The simple but intensely flavored dish is garnished with a pick-up-sticks design of julienned carrot and green onion.

INGREDIENTS

Four 5-ounce 'ōpakapaka fillets

Salt and freshly ground pepper to taste

1 cup fresh bread crumbs

1 tablespoon grated fresh ginger

2 large fresh cilantro sprigs, stemmed and minced (stems reserved)

3 cups water

2 jasmine tea bags

Coriander-Butter Sauce

1-1/2 tablespoons coriander seeds

2 tablespoons dry white wine

2 tablespoons plain rice wine vinegar

Reserved cilantro stems, above

1/4 cup heavy (whipping) cream

1 cup (2 sticks) unsalted butter, cut into tablespoon-sized pieces

Salt and freshly ground pepper to taste

Garnish

2 cups julienned green onions

1 carrot, peeled and cut into julienne

1 teaspoon finely diced fresh ginger

TO PREPARE THE FISH

Sprinkle the fish with salt and pepper. In a small bowl, combine the bread crumbs, ginger, and chopped cilantro.

continued on next page

Sprinkle this mixture over the fish. Put the fish in the top part of a steamer. In a small saucepan, bring the water to a boil. Set aside, add the tea, and steep for 3 minutes. Pour the tea into the bottom of the steamer, discarding the tea bags. Bring to a simmer, add the steamer section, cover, and steam for about 12 minutes, or until the fish flakes easily. Remove the fish from the pan and keep warm.

TO MAKE THE SAUCE

In a heavy, medium saucepan, combine the coriander seeds, white wine, vinegar, and cilantro stems. Cook over medium-high heat until reduced by half. Reduce heat to medium, add the heavy cream, and cook to reduce by half again. Reduce heat to low and whisk in the butter 1 tablespoon at a time. Strain through a fine-meshed sieve and season with salt and pepper.

TO SERVE

Place 1/4 cup of sauce on each plate and place 1 fillet in the center. Garnish the top of the fish with green onions and carrot, and sprinkle the ginger over the plate.

Alan Wong   *Alan Wong's Restaurant, Honolulu, O'ahu*

Sautéed Shrimp and Penne with Rice Cream Sauce

Serves 4

Penne pasta are topped with a creamy rice-based sauce studded with beautiful seared shrimp. The ingenious Alfredo-style sauce is made without cream, and the only butter is used as an enrichment for the shrimp. You may cut the quantity of the butter if you wish.

INGREDIENTS

Rice Cream Sauce

1 cup long-grain white rice

5-1/2 cups fish stock or clam juice

2-1/2 cups water

1 tablespoon olive oil

1 tablespoon minced garlic

1 tablespoon minced shallot

3/4 cup tomato water (recipe following)

1 cup dry white wine

4 cups chicken stock

1-1/2 tablespoons salt

24 large shrimp, peeled and deveined, tails left on

Salt and freshly ground pepper to taste

Flour for dredging

1/2 cup olive oil

2 teaspoons minced garlic

1/2 cup dry white wine

3/4 cup tomato water (recipe following)

2 teaspoons capers, drained

1/2 cup finely diced tomatoes

1/2 cup garlic-herb butter

4 tablespoons minced fresh Italian parsley

20 ounces penne pasta

Garnish

8 tablespoons grated Parmesan cheese

4 fresh basil sprigs

2 tomatoes, peeled, seeded, and chopped

Wash the rice. In a large saucepan, combine the rice, fish stock or clam juice, and water. Bring to a boil, then reduce heat to low and cook for 30 to 45 minutes, or until the liquid is absorbed and the rice is soft. Purée the rice in a blender or food processor until smooth.

In a large saucepan over medium-high heat, heat the oil and sauté the garlic and shallots for 2 minutes, until lightly browned and slightly translucent. Add the tomato water and white wine. Boil the mixture for 2 minutes, then add the chicken stock. When the stock boils, reduce heat to low and stir in the puréed rice. Add the salt and set aside.

Sprinkle the shrimp with salt and pepper and dredge lightly in flour. In a large sauté pan or skillet over medium-high heat, heat the olive oil until it ripples. Add the shrimp and sauté for 30 seconds on each side, or until golden. Add the garlic, wine, and tomato water, and stir to scrape up the browned bits from the bottom of the pan. Add the capers, tomatoes, garlic butter, parsley, and rice cream sauce. Cook and stir until the liquid has evaporated, 5 to 7 minutes. Season with salt and pepper.

Cook the pasta in a large pot of salted boiling water until al dente. Drain and toss with the shrimp sauce.

TO SERVE

Divide among 4 shallow bowls. Garnish each with 2 tablespoons of cheese and a basil sprig. Place a tablespoon of chopped tomato over center of each.

continued on next page

Tomato Water

8 vine-ripened tomatoes

Pinch of salt

PREPARATION

With a sharp, small knife, cut the unpeeled tomatoes
into chunks. Sprinkle with a pinch of salt and toss. Place the
tomato chunks in a fine-meshed sieve over a bowl, or wrap in
cheesecloth and place in a colander over a bowl. Refrigerate
overnight and let drip. A clear tomato liquid will collect in
the bowl. The tomato water may be used for subtle flavoring;
keep in a covered jar in the refrigerator up to 5 days.

George Mavrothalassitis   *Chef Mavro, Honolulu, O'ahu*

Papillotte of Kūmū with Basil, Seaweed, and Shiitake Mushrooms

Serves 4

Kūmū is a small member of the goatfish family, and like its cousins moano and weke, it's often fried whole. Steaming in parchment paper allows the fish to make its own sauce, enhanced by a surprising combination of ingredients.

INGREDIENTS

4 tablespoons extra-virgin olive oil

8 ounces shiitake mushrooms, stemmed and sliced

1 cup thinly sliced Maui or other sweet white onions

1-1/2 pounds kūmū or red snapper fillets, skin on

1 cup ogo (seaweed)

4 fresh basil sprigs, stemmed and minced

1/4 cup dry white wine

1/4 cup olive oil

1/4 cup fish stock, or clam juice mixed with 1/4 cup water

Salt and freshly ground pepper to taste

1 egg yolk, beaten

PREPARATION

In a medium sauté pan over medium-high heat, heat 2 tablespoons of the oil and sauté the mushrooms for 2 minutes, or until lightly browned on the edges. Remove the mushrooms from the pan and set aside. Heat the remaining oil in the pan and sauté the onions for 2 minutes, or until translucent. Set aside.

Preheat the oven to 450°F. Cut the fish into eight 1-inch-thick pieces. Cut 4 circles of parchment paper 14 inches in diameter. Fold the paper in half to make a center crease. Open the paper toward you and arrange the ingredients in the center: On 1 paper circle, layer one fourth of the onions, 2 fillets, and one fourth each of the mushrooms, ogo, basil, white wine, olive oil, and diluted fish stock. Salt and pepper to taste. Repeat with remaining 3 circles. Brush the inner edge of the paper with the beaten egg and fold the paper in half over theupward and back over themselves in 2-inch sections, sealing as you work and forming a twisted edge. Paper clip the final twist to hold tightly. It will look like a large tart.

Place the papillottes in a large, dry, ovenproof skillet over medium-high heat just until they begin to puff. Place the skillet in the oven and bake for 8 minutes. The parchment will puff slightly. With scissors, cut an opening in the parchment paper to allow the steam to escape. Serve the packages at the table.

Sam Choy   *Sam Choy's Restaurants of Hawai'i, Kailua-Kona, Hawai'i*

Crusted Mahimahi with Crab Bisque

Serves 4

The Japanese bread crumbs called panko give this dish very "island" flavor, and the coconut, spinach, and crab-meat in the bisque make it taste like a lū'au. The bisque is made of puréed taro leaves enriched with cream and coconut milk, forming a rich green halo around the fish.

INGREDIENTS

Mashed Purple Sweet Potatoes
1 pound Okinawan or regular sweet potatoes
1 cup hot milk
1 tablespoon unsalted butter
Salt and freshly ground pepper to taste

Crab Bisque
4 tablespoons unsalted butter
2 onions, diced
2 tablespoons flour
2 cups heavy (whipping) cream
1 cup coconut milk (see recipe on next page)
2 cups green taro leaves or frozen spinach, chopped
1-1/2 cups fresh lump crabmeat
Salt and freshly ground pepper to taste

Crusted Mahimahi
1 cup panko (Japanese bread crumbs)
1 cup macadamia nuts, finely chopped
1/2 cup minced fresh parsley
Four 8-ounce mahimahi fillets
Salt and freshly ground pepper to taste
1/2 cup all-purpose flour
2 eggs, lightly beaten
1/4 cup vegetable oil for frying

continued on next page

Sautéed Vegetables
2 tablespoons peanut oil

1 cup finely chopped onions

1 cup fresh bean sprouts

1/2 cup diagonally cut celery

5 ounces shiitake mushrooms, stemmed and sliced

3 ounces white mushrooms, sliced

1 red bell pepper, seeded, deribbed, and cut in julienne

Garnish
2 fresh cilantro sprigs

1 tablespoon black sesame seeds

Coconut Milk
freshly grated coconut meat from 1 coconut

TO MAKE COCONUT MILK
Place the coconut meat in a square of cheescloth. Bring the edges of the cheesecloth together and tie with a piece of string. Place the cheescloth bundle in a large pot. Bring enough water to cover the bundle to a boil in a separate pot, and pour over the coconut bundle. Let cool. When the water and coconut are cool enough to handle with your hands, squeeze the coconut milk through the cheescloth into the pot. Use immediately or refrigerate for up to 2 days.

TO MAKE THE POTATOES
Peel the sweet potatoes and cut into 1-inch dice. Cook the sweet potatoes in salted boiling water until tender, about 6 minutes. Drain. Combine the milk and butter and stir until

INGREDIENTS

Curry Sauce

2 tablespoons grated galangal or fresh ginger

3 lemongrass stalks, white part only

4 kaffir lime leaves, chopped

1 shallot

4 garlic cloves

2 tablespoons Thai chili paste

Ginger Beurre Blanc

1-1/2 cups dry white wine

2 tablespoons minced shallots

3 fresh parsley sprigs

3 white mushrooms, chopped

1/4 cup pickled ginger, cut into julienne

2 tablespoons heavy (whipping) cream

1 cup (2 sticks) unsalted butter, cut into tablespoon-
sized pieces

Salt and freshly ground pepper to taste

Noodle Cakes

2 pounds soba noodles

1/2 cup extra-virgin olive oil for frying

Six 6-ounce mahimahi fillets

Salt and freshly ground pepper to taste

1 cup cornstarch

1/4 cup extra-virgin olive oil

continued on next page

Spicy Stir-fried Vegetables
1 tablespoon Curry Sauce, above
1 red bell pepper, seeded, deribbed, and cut into julienne
1/4 cup white mushrooms, quartered
1/2 Maui or other sweet white onion, cut into julienne
1/4 bunch watercress, stemmed
1/2 cup fresh bean sprouts
1/4 cup Thai fish sauce

Garnish
2 tablespoons unsalted peanuts, chopped
1/4 cup fresh cilantro leaves, chopped

TO MAKE THE CURRY SAUCE

Grind all ingredients in a blender or a food processor until smooth. This can take 8 minutes or longer. Reserve or freeze until ready to use.

TO MAKE THE BEURRE BLANC

In a medium saucepan, combine the wine, shallots, parsley, mushrooms, and half of the pickled ginger. Cook over medium heat until almost evaporated. Add the cream and cook to reduce by half. Reduce heat to low and whisk in the butter 1 piece at a time. Remove the pan from the heat as necessary to keep the sauce just warm enough to melt each piece of butter. Remove from the heat and strain through a fine-meshed sieve. Add the remaining ginger, salt, and pepper. Keep warm over tepid water.

TO PREPARE THE NOODLE CAKES

Bring a large pot of water to boil over high heat. Add the noodles and let boil until just soft to the bite, about 6 minutes.

Drain in a colander. Divide the noodles into 6 equal portions. In a large sauté pan or skillet over medium-high heat, heat the oil until rippling. Add noodles, one portion at a time, pressing into a rectangle with the back of a spoon as they cook until they hold their shape. Cook on both sides until crisp and golden brown, about 3 minutes per side. Remove with a slotted spoon and drain on paper towels; set aside and keep warm. Repeat with remaining noodle portions.

Sprinkle the fillets with salt and pepper and coat them with cornstarch. In a large sauté pan or skillet over medium-high heat, heat the oil and cook the fillets for 3 minutes on each side, or until they flake easily and are golden brown.

TO MAKE THE STIR-FRIED VEGETABLES
Heat a wok over high heat, add the curry sauce, and stir-fry for 30 seconds. Add the bell pepper, mushrooms, onion, and watercress. Stir-fry for 1 minute. Add the bean sprouts and fish sauce. Set aside and keep warm.

TO SERVE
Place the noodle cakes at one end of a serving platter. Spoon the vegetables down the center of the platter, moving the red pepper strips to the top center of the vegetables. Spoon the beurre blanc over the vegetables, letting the sauce pool on the platter. Place 3 fillets on each side of the vegetables, touching in the center. Sprinkle with the peanuts and cilantro.

OnJin Kim   *OnJin's Cafe, Honolulu, O'ahu*

'Ōpakapaka with Sesame-Chili Sauce

Serves 4

A halo of fresh asparagus and a flavorful sauce made with ginger and chili make a healthful dish look and taste spectacular. At heart, this is a simple fillet of perfectly cooked fish.

INGREDIENTS

24 asparagus stalks

Four 6-ounce 'ōpakapaka or other mild white fleshed
 fish fillets

1/2 cup Asian sesame oil

1 teaspoon minced fresh ginger

1 Hawaiian or Thai chili, finely diced, or 1 pinch of red
 pepper flakes

2 tablespoons finely chopped green onion, white part only

1/4 cup soy sauce

8 fresh cilantro sprigs, stemmed

PREPARATION

Holding an asparagus stalk in your hands, bend it until it
snaps off. Discard the tough lower end. With a sharp, small
knife, score the skin of the fish in a criss-cross pattern. Place
the asparagus and 'ōpakapaka over simmering water in a
covered steamer for 5 minutes, until the fish is opaque on
the outside but translucent in the center. The asparagus
will be crisp-tender.

In a sauté pan or skillet over high heat, heat the oil and sauté
the ginger, chili, and 1 tablespoon of the green onions for 12
seconds. Add the soy sauce and bring to a boil.

TO SERVE

Place a fillet in the center of each serving plate. Pour the
sauce over the fish fillets. Place 6 asparagus stalks single file
around each plate, overlapping the tip of one over the lower
end of the next. Garnish the fish with the cilantro sprigs and
remaining 1 tablespoon green onion.

Glossary of Ingredients

A

'Ahi:
The Hawaiian name for both yellowfin and big eye tuna. Often served in the islands as sashimi (Japanese-style raw fish).

Asian sesame oil:
A strong-flavored oil made from toasted sesame seeds and used in most Asian cuisines. Only a small amount is needed for flavoring. Sesame oil burns at a lower heat than most oils. Refrigerate after opening.

B

Bean sprouts:
Mung beans that have sprouted. Available fresh or canned.

Black Sesame Seeds:
Also called goma. Available in bottles or packages in Asian markets.

Breadfruit:
A bland, starchy vegetable widely used in the Pacific, but difficult to get on the U.S. mainland. Potatoes are a good substitute.

C

Chili paste:
A thick chili sauce produced and used in many Asian cuisines such as Thai, Vietnamese, Indonesian, and Filipino. It is made of chilis, onions, sugar, and tamarind.

Chili pepper water:
A hot mixture of small red chilies, salt, vinegar, and garlic. It may be purchased in bottle form or see the recipe on page 28.

Chinese cabbage:
See won bok.

Chinese long rice:
See bean thread noodles.

Chinese mustard cabbage:
Also known as gai choy; mustard greens may be substituted.

Chinese parsley:
See cilantro.

Cilantro:
A pungent flat-leaf herb resembling parsley; also called fresh coriander or Chinese parsley.

Coconut milk:
A liquid extracted from shredded coconut meat by soaking it with hot water and straining. Available in cans from Southeast Asia, or see the recipe on page 66.

D

Daikon:
Japanese name for a white, crisp radish. Turnips can be substituted.

F

Fish sauce:
Also called nam pla in Thai cuisine or nuoc mam in Vietnamese cuisine. Very salty and pungent. Made from fermented small fish and shrimp. Available in Asian markets.

G

Galangal:
Also called Thai ginger or galangha. A large, juicy rhizome with a thin pinkish-brown skin. Substitute fresh ginger.

Ginger:
Fresh ginger is a brown, fibrous, knobby rhizome. It keeps for long periods of time. To use, peel the brown skin and slice, chop, or puree. It will keep indefinitely placed in a jar with sherry and refrigerated.

Goma:
See black sesame seeds.

Gyoza:
A Japanese dumpling, also known as a pot sticker.

H

Hāhā:
The Hawaiian word for the stem of the taro plant. See taro.

Hawaiian salt:
A coarse sea salt gathered in tidal pools after a storm or high tide. Hawaiians sometimes mix it with a red clay to make alae salt. Substitute kosher salt.

I

Ichimi:
See togarishi.

Imu:
A firepit, or underground oven of hot volcanic stones, used in Hawaiian cooking to steam food.

J

Japanese eggplant:
A long, narrow, purple eggplant. Substitute Italian eggplant.

Jasmine rice:
A fragrant and delicate Asian rice. Substitute white long-grained rice.

K

Kaffir lime leaves:
Citrus-flavored leaves sold in Asian markets. Used widely in Southeast Asian dishes. Sold fresh or dried. Reconstitute dried leaves by soaking in warm water. Substitute grated lime zest.

Kajiki:
The Japanese name for Pacific blue marlin. Substitute swordfish or shark.

Kalo:
The Hawaiian word for taro root. See taro.

Kālua pig:
Shredded pork that has been cooked in a traditional underground pit, or imu.

Kecap manis:
A thick, dark Indonesian soy sauce sweetened with palm sugar. Available in Asian markets.

Kukui nuts:
A native Hawaiian nut very high in oil. Used roasted, salted, or pounded in traditional Hawaiian cooking.

Kūmū:
A reef fish and a member of the goatfish family. Its meat is mild and delicate. Substitute any white meat fish with a high fat content, such as flounder or halibut.

L

Lemongrass:
Long greenish stalks with a pungent lemony flavor. Also called citronella. Substitute grated lemon zest.

Liliko'i:
The Hawaiian name for passion fruit, which is a small yellow, purple, or brown oval fruit of the passion fruit vine. The "passion" in passion fruit comes from the fact that its flower resembles a Maltese cross and refers to Christ's crucifixion, not to aphrodesiac qualities. The flavor is delicate but somewhat sharp, and perfume-like. Passion fruit is a natural substitute for lemon juice. Passion fruit concentrate can be found in the frozen juice section of many markets. Substitute oranges.

Limu:
The Hawaiian word for seaweed, of which they use as many as twenty-five varieties. Japanese ogo is a type of seaweed. Much ogo today is farm raised.

Lū'au:
A traditional Hawaiian feast that usually includes foods prepared in an imu, or underground oven. See page 8.

Lū'au Leaves:
    The young, green tops
    of the taro root. Substitute
    fresh spinach.

Lumpia wrappers:
    Thin rectangular noodle sheets
    used to make lumpia, the
    Filipino version of pot stickers.
    Substitute eggroll skins.

Lychee:
    A small fruit with white meat
    and a hard shell. Available fresh
    and canned in Asian markets.

....

M

Macadamia nuts:
    A rich, oily nut grown mostly on
    the Big Island of Hawai'i. Native
    to Australia. They're good, but
    expensive, canned.

Macadamia nut oil:
    A premium cooking and salad
    oil produced in Hawaii from
    macadamia nuts. It has a high
    heat threshold for burning.

Mahimahi:
    Also called dolphinfish, with a
    firm, pink flesh. Best fresh,
    but often available frozen. A
    standard in island restaurants
    and markets. Substitute snap-
    per, catfish, or halibut.

Mango:
    Gold and green tropical fruit
    available in many supermarkets.
    Available fresh June through
    September in Hawai'i.
    Substitute fresh peaches.

Maui onion:
    A very sweet, juicy, large round
    onion similiar to the Vidalia or
    Walla Walla onion. Often
    available on the West Coast, but
    expensive. Substitute any
    sweet white onion.

Mirin:
    A sweet Japanese rice wine
    found in Asian markets.
    Substitute sweet sherry.

....

N

Nam pla:
    See fish sauce.

Napa cabbage:
    See won bok.

Noodles:
    Rice stick noodles:
    Thin rice noodles usually sold
    coiled in the package. When
    dropped into hot oil they puff
    up into cruchy sticks.

    **Soba Japanese buckwheat flour
    noodles:**
    Soba noodles are light
    brown and thin. They are eaten
    warm or cold.

O

Ogo:
The Japanese name for seaweed.

Opah:
A very large moonfish. Substitute swordfish.

Okinawan sweet potato:
A sweet potato with purple flesh. Substitute any yam or sweet potato.

ʻŌpakapaka:
A pink snapper with a delicate flavor. Good poached, baked or sautéed. Substitute any red snapper, sea bass, or monkfish.

Oyster Sauce:
A concentrated sauce made from oyster juice and salt, used in many Chinese and other Asian dishes. Keeps a long time in the refrigerator.

P

Panko:
A crispy, large-flaked Japanese bread crumb that adds more texture than ordinary bread crumbs. Found in Asian markets.

Passion fruit:
See liliko'i. Passion fruit juice concentrate can be found in the frozen juice section of some markets. Substitute orange juice concentrate.

Patis fish sauce:
A strong-flavored seasoning sauce used in Southeast Asian cuisines. Tiparos® is one brand name.

Pineapple:
Fresh pineapples are covered with a prickly brown skin, and topped with sharp, pointed leaves. To select a fresh ripe pineapple, give the tiny center leaves at the top a light tug: The leaves will easily pluck out of a ripe pineapple. Fresh pineapple contains an enzyme which will break down protein; rinse well and add as close to serving time as possible when using in dishes containing gelatin.

Puna goat cheese:
A fresh white goat cheese produced in the Puna district of the island of Hawaiʻi. It is made in the traditional French way. Substitute any fresh white goat cheese.

Purple potatoes:
See Okinawan sweet potatoes.

R

Rice noodles:
Also called rice vermicelli. When they are deep-fried they expand immediately to several

times their size. They can also be soaked and served as soft noodles. Packages of the dry noodles are in Asian markets.

Rice wine vinegar:
A light vinegar made from fermented rice.

S

Sake:
Clear Japanese rice wine. Other strong clear liquors, such as tequila or vodka, can be substituted.

Sesame seeds:
Small, flat, oval, white or black seeds used to flavor or garnish main dishes and desserts.

Shichimi:
A Japanese spice blend of chilies, sesame seeds, orange peel, seaweed, and poppy seeds. Substitute Cajun spice mix.

Shiitake mushrooms:
The second most widely cultivated mushroom in the world, medium to large with umbrella-shaped, flopped tan to dark brown caps with edges that tend to roll under. Shiitakes have a woodsy, smoky flavor. Can be purchased fresh or dried in Asian groceries. To reconstitute the dried variety, soak in warm water for 30 minutes before using. Stem both fresh and dried shiitakes.

Shoyu:
The Japanese and Hawaiian name for soy sauce.

Shutome:
The Hawaiian broadbill swordfish. Substitute any swordfish.

Soba noodles:
Thin, brown noodles made from buckwheat and wheat flour. They cook quickly and can be served hot or cold.

Soy Sauce:
A dark salty liquid made from soybeans, flour, salt, and water. Dark soy sauce is stronger than light soy sauce. A staple in most Asian cuisines.

Sprouts:
Bean, daikon, pea, sunflower, and radish are all types of sprouts used in salads and vegetable dishes in Hawai'i. Most can be found in Asian or natural foods stores.

Star Anise:
Brownish seeds with eight points that taste like licorice.

Star fruit:
A waxy, light green fruit; also called carambola. Cut in cross section, it reveals a five-pointed star shape. Trim the points off the stars if the points are too dark for your taste.

Sweet chili sauce:
   See Thai chili paste.

T

Tamarind:
   A brown, bean-shaped pod from the tamarind tree. The fruit is sweet-sour, and is made into sauces, candy, and pastes.

Taro:
   A starchy root of the taro, called kalo, is pounded to make poi. Its flavor is similar to artichokes or chestnuts. The leaves (lūʻau) and stems (hāhā) are also used in cooking. Taro contains an irritating substance and must be cooked before any part of the plant can be eaten.

Taro leaves:
   See lūʻau leaves.

Thai chili paste:
   A slightly sweet, thick, hot, bottled paste of garlic, vinegar, and chilies. Sriracha® is a brand name.

Tiparos® fish sauce:
   A brand of bottled Filipino fish sauce used to season many Asian dishes.

Tobiko:
   The orange roe of the flying fish. Similar to caviar, it has a mild flavor and slight crunch. It is available in red, black, and green in Japanese markets.

Togarashi:
   Japanese red pepper flakes, also called ichimi. Substitute red pepper flakes.

W

Warabi:
   See fiddlehead ferns.

Won bok:
   Cabbage-like vegetable, also called napa or Chinese cabbage.

Wonton wrappers:
   Thin sheets of noodle dough used to wrap food for frying or steaming.

For a listing of mail order sources for various ingredients check our website *www.mutualpublishing.com.*